High Paraguai
and the
Swamps of Araguaia

ISBN: 9781694437563

High Paraguai
and the
Swamps of Araguaia

JUAN SANZ SANZ

CLARIFICATION:

In 1984, after years of thorough studies, many calculations and checks, JUAN SANZ SANZ (1943 - 2019), announced, before two of the high levels of the great country that is Brazil, privately and personally, two different projects that He presented them with the following titles: IDEAS FOR A DESICCATION PROJECT AND CULTIVATION OF THE SWAMPS OF HIGH PARAGUAI and AVENATION OF SWAMPS THE ARAGUAIA RIVER.

The magnitude of the works that he proposed in them indicated to the author the correct way to go and he was not mistaken, the two estates of the State contacted by him did not delay the formal answers.

Unfortunately, the very cultured man has just passed away, a self-taught man who many would not hesitate to describe as a prototype of a person close to the Renaissance, given the large amount of knowledge that he sought to enlarge throughout his existence.

The baggage provided by his wisdom, due to the depth of the immersion he made for decades in

Geography and History, together with the careful observation of how much was happening in those years throughout the planet, they then gave the ill-fated author the necessary impulse to develop his work.

It is good to remember again that we speak of 1984, so, as in this 21st century, the word weighed heavily against him, always present in a hierarchical excess society: SELF-TAUGHT.

Now, without moving a comma from his legacy, his Water Projects are published for the first time; the one that corresponds to Brazil is titled, so leave the author decided to save the files that contain them: HIGH PARAGUAI and the SWAMPS of ARAGUAIA.

BIOGRAPHY:

Self-taught, Juan Sanz Sanz (1943-2019), devoted himself, from early youth, to unravelling the problems posed by the readings of historical events narrated by the various authors who frequently diverged from each other.

Geography was one of his great hobbies and reason for fervent study, not existing on the planet place, no matter how remote it was, that had not been fully informed.

The attentive follow-up of the social and political reality in which its existence took place resulted in proposals for water use on three continents and each of the projects was sent in its day to the places that were most suitable for its achievement.

Languages - French, English, Italian, Portuguese and German, in addition to his own, Spanish - had no secrets for him and thus he could fully enjoy the Literature written in them, another hobby in which, as an enlightened man, he found his peers.

In early youth the Spanish guitar and later the piano, were musical instruments to which he dedicated a great effort similar to the passion that the music awoke in him and thus, in maturity, with authentic devotion and delicacy, he interpreted beautiful pieces of Bach , Chopin, Debussy and Beethoven who contributed a lot to make their days more human and the passage of time milder.

In addition to the Water Projects, it leaves literary works practically about to be edited, something that will be sought in public light.

In memoriam

INTRODUCTION:

1984

The problem of Brazil is similar in nature to that of China. It is a very large State (8.5 Mkm2), very populated (130 Mhb), with great potential resources, huge forests, the largest river in the world and a very old settlement, since the beginning of the discovery of the New World. In the past it was important for its gold mines, for the dye plant that gave it its name, for its sugar plantations. But the colonial system is based on a duplicity. There are two completely different societies that they coexist apparently in the same territory. A very advanced society, which lives up to the most advanced of each era, and a huge territory, completely out of it. Hence, these theoretical borders only contain, in reality, a commercial space in which the products of the State can circulate more easily than outside the borders. But what value does this really have? The "national territory" is nothing more than a border, a limit, which has no more value than that of its customs posts with respect to other borders. Theoretically citizens can move through it unhindered, but this is the theory; In reality, there are no borders there.

Therefore, Brazil does not end in the confines of the Amazon, but in the densely populated regions of the Mato Grosso. This is the first interesting fact that we must highlight. South America is a world without borders, like Africa. In South America there are not even linguistic differences that slow down migration, since the affinity between Portuguese and Spanish is such that it is reduced to accent.

Brazil is thus formed by two different realities, strange - in a way - with each other: a densely populated territory and a vast semi-empty space.

The contrast is very pronounced, although here we do not find large alluvial plains densely cultivated as in Asia. The concentrated South American population is located in large cities, because its character is mixed - industrial and agricultural. The colonial system is based on the juxtaposition of two almost incommunicado societies. One is not an extension of the other, but they are two different realities. This fact is not exclusive to Brazil, but to all of South America and part of Asia. There is a nucleus with very dense population and cultural level integrated in the modern life, and a periphery, many times more extensive.

This is the first and most serious imbalance that colonial societies suffer - not because they are colonies, but because their structure remains colonial. Despite this, and even if it hurts patriotism, to what extent are they still colonies of other metropolises? Whose colony is the colonized part of Brazil? There is no doubt about the countries that facilitate its economic development. We must not forget that before the Independence, the country had a very special situation with respect to its metropolis, a unique case.

Portugal was not a great power and Brazil was too big. Thus, the colony had greater weight than the metropolis from the 17th century. That is why independence came naturally without shock. The greatest glory of Portugal has undoubtedly been the formation of the Brazilian colony. The enormity of the territories that Portugal administered on the eastern coast of South America made the metropolis represent only the unitary factor, especially the military power capable of preventing disintegration. All this would not have been possible, however, without British help, to whom this situation always agreed.

There was the anomalous case here that the colony, in the century before independence, had more economic power and more population than the metropolis, made unusual in European colonial history. It is a singularity that remained for centuries. After independence, Portugal and Brazil have never become antagonistic. Thus, between Spain and its former colonies a great period of time (almost a century and a half) has had to pass before the antagonism is diluted and forgotten. Let's not forget that the independence of Spanish and English-speaking America occurred traumatically, as a result of bloody wars, while Brazil, like Canada, has separated from its metropolis peacefully. The ancient links of affinity and sympathy were not clouded by the hatred and violence of the ortho of those nations. One of the most interesting events that are occurring in recent times, in this sense, is a reconciliation of Spain with its former colonies. On the other hand, the British colonies in the New World - I refer exclusively to the United States - and the old metropolis, past the time of mutual resentment, has moved into an attitude of rivalry and alliance. They are two great powers and the old metropolis is not resigned to recognize the superiority of the colony.

Between Spain and the Spanish-speaking countries of America there is no longer that resentment, nor can there be a rivalry, since none are great powers in the world concert. But between Brazil and Portugal, not only has there been no rivalry, but no resentment. This gives Brazilian history a remarkable particularity. Its bloodless origin is nothing more than a manifestation of its stable and balanced history. It is another notable fact that should be highlighted, because it explains the maintenance of the Brazilian unit, despite its enormous extent and diversity. Indeed, Spanish-speaking

States have an origin war they have emerged from a war of independence; military power has always been decisive. The unity of the huge Brazilian territory has been possible because the state substrate was concord, stability. Brazil has not had the handicap suffered by the other part of America that became peacefully independent, Canada. In Brazil there is nothing similar.

All this has been the past and explains the existence of Brazilian unity, in contrast to the fragmentation of America of Spanish origin. In the same way that we can explain ourselves to American unity by the pragmatic spirit of collaboration that is imposed on personal matters.

Despite their rivalries, the American colonies knew how to associate with each other, since it was more what united them than what separated them. This enviable spirit does not exist in Spanish-speaking America. That pragmatism does not exist there; instead, if in Brazil. It is remarkable that spirit of fragmentation, of cantonalism that exists in our people, in contrast to the conciliatory and utilitarian spirit of others. Among us, personal issues, which are hardly subject to interest voluntarily, are the determining factor.

The Brazilian nation has emerged with another spirit; hence its great stability.

However, in our time new factors are appearing that threaten to spoil this enviable situation. Population growth is forcing societies to transform at a dizzying pace to meet the demand of these masses that appear in the labour market, whose subsistence needs must be met.

Hence, traditional Brazilian stability threatens to become serious instability if this problem cannot be resolved. The successive military governments in recent decades and the rise of the importance of the military factor within Brazilian society are symptomatic, not to maintain a unit that is not threatened, but to contain this irresistible growth in social demand, to which no full satisfaction is achieved. This is a problem of very difficult solution, aggravated by the abysmal financial crisis that is suffered today, which has ended with the hope of a solution through rapid industrialization.

It is a very serious situation, which we will analyse later in depth, whose first consequence is the lack of food, the danger of serious famines that threaten that mass of 130 million people (1984 data)

This is the most serious, most urgent problem. It is necessary to increase the production capacity of livelihoods to prevent a very serious situation, now that it is still time, and in this sense we offer this possibility of colonization of this alluvial space that perhaps can be put into cultivation.

TERRITORY:

PARAGUAI RIVER

The Paraguai River, near its sources, enters the vast Pantanal, whose altitude is 107 meters in Porto Esperança, at the railroad crossing. A vast region of 300 km. for 400 km. It is flooded. The height of normal floods is 4 to 5 meters. The exceptional ones reach 7 meters and flood the entire swamp. The rise of the waters is regular and late; the water level rises slowly and remains relatively low during the first months of rains (November-December).

The flood begins in December and the waters rise until May-June, a month or two after the rainy season. Only then does the flood spread rapidly down. The tracks of the plains are no longer passable.

Here we observe a phenomenon of strangulation of the valley, which causes the hills that the railroad takes advantage of. Lower of them, the swamps follow both sides of the river, but less extensive. Between the Bodoquena mountain range and the Corumbé massif the river is strangled. This explains the strange phenomenon that until the swamp does not fill, it does not begin to flow down; in turn, that the flood is not noticed until some times after the rains.

ARAGUAIA RIVER

The Tocantins or Pará river has a length of 2,700 km. Its main tributary, which forms the parallel valley, is the Araguaia, a river born in the mountains of Mato Grosso. The Araguaia valley has, from its sources to the confluence of the Tocantins, a straight-line length of 1,500 km. The average width is 200 km; therefore, the extension of about 300,000 km2. The average rains are 1 to 2 ms, closer to this amount than the first. Therefore, the flow rate must be 3,000 to 4,000 m3 / s.

The region that interests us is the middle valley of the Araguaia, El Bananal, a region of about 500 km long along the river, covered with floodplains in the middle of the Brazilian plateau, which generally lacks rich and deep soils. A navigable section is formed here, since the Tocantins valley barely serves as a navigation route. Upon entering this basin, the Araguaia is divided into two arms, forming a vast interior delta 300 km long. There is a major arm, to the west, and a minor arm, joined together by channels.

Further down, the course of the two joined arms crosses numerous streams and is only navigable again in the region of the confluence with the Tocantins.

The plain of the Araguaia, is of sandy and poor floods. Here, the riparian forest is nothing more than a narrow gallery after which the savanna with scrubland alternates with palm groves.

But this refers to the upper part of the plain, towards 13 and 14 latitude. To the E. of this area extends one of the largest forest masses, to the N. of Goias, in the mountains that separate the

Araguaia basin from those of the
upper Tocantins.

THE HIGH XINGU

The Xingu and the Araguaia cross regions that form sedimentary coverts in archaic shields, similar to the plains of Mojos, and the Río de la Plata basin as a whole. Now, these sediments, what value do they really have? The Sahara, Arabia, Russia, Eastern Siberia, are covered with such formations. This does not mean that they are fertile floods.

In the High Xingu there is a swampy region, similar to that of the Araguaia, caused, no doubt by the floods that interrupt its course below. This river flows into the Amazon at the point where the great river begins its delta. Its navigable section does not reach 200 km (180 km), when its total course is 1,980 km. Along the channel, no less than 8 streams can be counted on the map.

The four enclaves of Madeira, Paraguai, Xingu and Araguaia are contiguous, forming a kind of continuous strip from Beni to Araguaia: 2,000 km, 100,000 km2 in the plains of Moxos; 100,000 in the upper Paraguai; 50,000 in the Araguaia; in total, 300,000 km2, 30 million hectares.

One thing that intrigues is the kind of land in the Paraná region, between this river and the Mato

Grosso, almost uninhabited today. It is evident that the amount of arable land is reduced in Brazil. In this territory the vegetation is the tropical savanna. The truth is that Brazilian peasants have eagerly sought new lands to colonize throughout their country.

THE MATO GROSSO

The 1977 was segregated from the State of Mato Grosso that of Mato Grosso do Sul. This has 350,000 km2 and 1.5 Mhb (1984), with capital in Campo Grande (150), city on the Bolivian railway, halfway between the Paraguai and Paraná rivers. The remainder of Mato Grosso is 880,000 km2 and 1 Mhb (1984) alone, of which 0.8 live the capital, Cuiaba, in the northern part of the swamps. In the rest of that huge territory only 200,000 people live. The urban growth of Cuiaba, if the data is credible, is incredible.

In 1970 it had 105,000 inhabitants, in 1975, 765,000; this last fact is, then, that of 1975. The influx of capitals must have turned this city into the center of an industrial exploitation of the territory. It is not strange, since this one includes the swamps of the Paraguai, to the South, and the jungles until the parallel 10, to the N. DE there the name of Big Forest. A narrow strip of low mountains between the swamps and the jungle.

Rains fall during the southern summer, between October and April. The dry season is quite pronounced, between May and September.

In Cuiaba, rainfall is zero between June and August. There is intense radiation during the night in the dry season (southern winter) and the temperature drops to 2 degrees; Daily oscillations reach 24 degrees.

A large part of the plateau is covered by slightly inclined sandstone platforms, called "plated", which are interrupted in length, leaving the base of crystalline rocks to appear. The fronts of the sandstone plateaus form alignments of high rocky cliffs, proceeding from elevations isolated, fragments separated from those by erosion.

Below the level of the "plated" circular reception basins are formed. Where water and working land abound; there the haciendas and the cities are installed.

On the upper Paraguai basin the plateau brake is marked by a huge escarpment of 200 to 400 meters, in which red sandstones are associated with basalts; It is oriented to the N., from Aquidauana to N. de Cuiabá (about 700 km); then twist the O. by the Serra dos Parecis to the Madeira.

The Xingu forms, between 13 and 10 ° S, before leaving the area of sandstones, a quiet stretch, describing meanders in a plain covered with sandy alluviums, between ridges of 2 to 8 meters, above which the Great flood waters.

It is a tropical savanna climate. In summer, the mass of equatorial air, full of moisture, dominates, with a sky constantly covered with large clusters, which cause frequent rains. When, in the middle of summer, southern air masses arrive, heavy rains and floods occur.

The average rains are 1,800 mm, of which fall in summer between 1,600 and 1,700.

In winter, air masses from the South Atlantic penetrate, light and stable winds, with little cloudiness; The sky is almost always clear. Sometimes fresh air penetrates. The difference between night and daytime temperatures can reach 30º, although it is always hot during the day.

Predominates what is called "closed field" there, grassland of hard and spaced grasses, dotted with trees. The soil is even poorer than that of the "kills", because the amount of organic material is almost nil, from 1 to 1.5%. This is the "plated".

In the valleys the closed field is replaced by the forest, especially on the banks of the rivers, with characters similar to the Amazon forest. In the sources of the rivers these forests disappear.

On the slopes of the headwaters the "clean field" predominates, grassland without trees.

Between the 13th and 14th, the Araguaia plain is covered with sandy and poor floods.

CONSIDERATIONS:

The problem we are trying to solve is the possibility of replacing jungle vegetation with cultivated plant vegetation, with plantations. It has been done in Southeast Asia - Malaysia, Java, Sumatra. In these countries it rains all year round, the dry season is barely noticeable. In the Amazon the climate is constant and humid. The problem is, as I say, replace that natural vegetation with another one cultivated. In such a situation, everything depends on the fertility of the soil. The jungle sustains itself, as the extreme abundance of rains she is holding a vegetation, which grows quickly, and the remains of this vegetation maintain the richness of the soil. That is, the spontaneous subscriber is produced by the fall to the ground of branches, leaves, trunks of trees and shrubs. Its decomposition provides the soil with humus. And this occurs even if there is hardly any mineral cover, earth. The forest grows on the living rock, provided there is a minimum of decomposed rock where the roots can ignite. Its growth is promoted by the decomposition of the forest itself.

It is a closed cycle and, therefore, when the forest is cut down, it can no longer be renewed. Breaking that balance can be a dangerous thing, because it is difficult for him to rebuild again. This occurs, in general, in all forests, not only in equatorial forests. Forests give a deceptive impression of exuberance and fertility. Its plant wealth has been achieved over a long time, after an internal evolution in which fertility has been growing. If the forest is destroyed, whose evolution has lasted many successive generations of trees, a cycle begins in the opposite direction.

That is why it is necessary to take into account that replacing the forest with the plantation produces an irremediable transformation. Large forests have been created by Nature in the course of thousands of years and their partial destruction should only be done when it is really necessary, because it is irreversible. Once this is done, let's return to the possibility of cultivating regions that are much less fertile than it seems at first glance. We are dazzled by the luxuriant richness of the forest with trees of 50 and 60 meters, with several floors of vegetation.

The forest is like a greenhouse; cutting down trees is like opening holes in it: the ecosystem is destroyed. That is why they should only be tried if it is really possible and necessary.

In the Amazon, the problem is trying to take advantage of the firm lands, outside of the floods, which are those that can be used without risks and without prior conditioning work. But really, what is the soil of these lands? The explorations have made little progress in this regard.

However, what is evident is that tertiary floods are what predominate in the Amazon. The enormous body of water has produced the formation of channels of great strength, which remain foreign to the rest, and only on its banks do we find Quaternary floods.

The Ganges Valley has similar conditions. The plain between the Himalayas and the archaic massif of Gonwana was filled, in the same way as the plain between the Andes and the Guiana-Brazilian massif. However, what are the differences? Because, in summary, what happens is that geologically the forest has been very little explored, at least at the time (1960) since it was an insurmountable obstacle.

1984

DETAILED STUDY

HIGH PARAGUAI
AND THE
SWAMPS OF ARAGUAIA

JUAN SANZ SANZ

ONE

You can empty a territory in two ways: deepening the levels or widening the channels, or an action of both. It would not be necessary to deepen the Paraguai channel so much if its channel were extended, giving greater ease at the exit of the annual flood. The slope in the swamps is certainly very small, but the water outlet is contained by some natural obstacles, and this is usually a determining cause. In the case of High Paraguai, it is the strangulation suffered by the channel between the Sierra Bodoquena and the Corumba massif.

The altitude of El Pantanal, as this territory is called, is only 107 meters, according to the measures taken during the construction of the Northwest railway, from Sao Paulo to Bolivia. Therefore, a very low height. If we are to pay attention to the map, the level of 100 meters above sea level is 150 km north of Asunción and 500 km south of these strangulations. If it is possible or not, it is something that I cannot determine. One thing, however, is quite clear: the waters would not stay here for most of the rainy season if they had a natural exit and this is is the work that the human industry should execute.

The cause of the Pantanal is none other than that narrowing of the channel, which forms a natural dam. Simply cancel it so that the waters have an exit.

TWO

The case of High Paraguai is one of the most notable examples of natural water reservoirs of large rivers due to the lack of unevenness and the lack of exit. However, it is not only the lack of general unevenness, but local that matters. In Africa, whose coastal part is raised by old mountains, this phenomenon occurs with relative frequency, Thus, the Nile in the marshes of the Sedd; Congo, in the swamps above Kinshasa; the Niger in the Macina or the Zambeze in the swamps of the Barotse, are notable examples.

Here the cause of the narrowing of the riverbed, which contains the flooded waters above the streams, eventually producing, after ages, a flat and muddy plain. In others, cases is the lack of unevenness. So it is in the mighty Yangzi, although there are no obstructions in its channel. Recall that Yichang is only 40 ms above the sea, and at a distance of 1,800 km from the mouth. It is enough that further under Wuhan the channel narrows somewhat so that the river is not able to give way to the general flood. Water is deposited and sediments gradually increase the level of the water plain.

Thus we find the great swamps of the middle course region of the river. The strength of the monsoon flood, the lack of unevenness, the narrowing of the channel a little lower and the elevation of the plain due to sedimentation are sufficient causes for this phenomenon to occur. The same can be said of the Menam, the river of Thailand, whose narrowing in the middle course region is the cause of the northern part of the plain being an impracticable swamp. Similarly, the great swamps of western Siberia are due to the lack of unevenness of the plain.

The case of High Paraguai is one of the most notable, since they occur at a great distance from the mouth. It is, perhaps, the region of permanent swamps located more distance from the sea.

THREE

The plain of the High Paraguai forms like a sea gulf between ancient massifs that has been clogged throughout the ages. To the North, the Serra dos Parecis; to E, the plateau of Mato Grosso; to the O, the low massif of the plains of Chiquitos. These last two tend to unite and form the narrowing of the Corumba region. These mountains, generally of low elevation, fall, however, to peak on the plain, in successive steps, forming true cliffs, especially that of the eastern part. An almost continuous line of cliffs follows the plain for hundreds of kilometres, only interrupted by the gaps that the rivers open when it flows into it.

Now, the problem that arises is the following; If the sediments deposited in the plain come from surrounding mountains and these are generally sandstones, what type of floods have formed there?

I lack the elementary knowledge to know. Happy specialists, who seem to know everything and whose knowledge is useful for so little. But large herbs grow here, there is abundant livestock. The floods have to be fertile.

FOUR

It is also necessary to ask why such a simple thing has not been done so far. This region has recently become a nature reserve. With this, no economic activity can be developed there. Logically, these decisions cannot be final, but they have, instead, quite a lot of significance. They indicate that the Brazilian government has no agricultural and industrial projects on this territory. That means two things: or that this possibility has not occurred to them - drainage and cultivation - or that, once examined, it is not possible to put it into practic

It is unlikely that the restless Brazilian spirit has not fixed attention on these potentially arable lands.

Brazil is a "gigantic", "immense" country - all the appellants have been applied to it - but it lacks extensive agricultural spaces. His neighbour Argentina has them almost in excess. In Brazil, only a small part of the territory is arable and that is why an enclave like this, of 80,000 km2, has exceptional value. The great Amazonian plains are formed by ancient floods of gravels and sandstones and their cultivation is difficult.

On the plateau, the mountains leave few large spaces to which tractors can be applied.

For that reason, being evident the existence of that great alluvial territory and having that country, with its 130 million mouths to feed (1984), so much need of it, it is still strange that, or this possibility has not been raised or has been discarded, since its transformation into a nature reserve proves it. In this case, we have to think of two possibilities: either the project has insurmountable technical problems or, simply, it has not occurred to them.

However, this second possibility seems, at first glance, more remote. It is unlikely that having a great city like Cuiaba on its banks, it has been so blind.

However, we cannot lose sight of a fact. On the one hand, the Paraguai River, as soon as it leaves the swamps, enters foreign territory. There are two routes that border it: on the North, the road that from the coast reaches the heart of the Mato Grosso; by the South, the railroad of the Northwest. Within the Pantanal there are no roads, no railroads, no cities or villages.

It is a great desert, a stain, an obstacle to avoid by travellers except ornithologists. It is something we should not lose sight of. But there is something even more important: the magnitude of the project itself. The drainage works would be somewhat colossal and until recent times impracticable. We must not forget that we are in a new technological situation. Current engineering has much more powerful means than immediate generations. The capacity of traction, of drag, of machines and instruments has multiplied.

In a place not far from that, the gigantic Itapu reservoir has been built, but it is only a dike. Perhaps the current mentality has not yet adapted to the action of these instruments, although some have long been in operation.

On the other hand, you should not forget that the Brazilian mentality has changed in recent times. Before it was oriented towards the inner border, to the conquest of the great deserted, jungle spaces, which promised wealth of very doubtful extraction. Now Brazil is a country troubled by multiple problems.

His concern and action is focused on large cities, in densely populated regions of the coast. It is here where the immediate problems are and, perhaps, blinded by it, the current Brazilians do not realize that solutions often arise in the most unexpected way. Because we face the eternal problem of the vicious circle and it can only be broken by introducing new elements into it. If the drainage of this vast empty region is possible, the many millions of hectares of arable land it contains could be a decisive factor in breaking it.

FIVE

"The height of normal floods is 4 to 5 meters in Corumba. The exceptional ones reach 7 meters and flood the entire swamp. The rise of the waters is remarkably regular and late. During all the time in which the water can continue to spread, its level rises slowly. The waters remain low during the first months of rains (November-December). The flood begins in December and the waters rise until May or June, one or two months after the end of the rainy season. Only then they cease to be passable during the flood."

"In the low zone with flooded grasslands alternate spots of poor forest. Floating meadows called "*camalotes*" are formed in depressions occupied by bathes. The gallery forests follow the river courses only at the top."

"In El Pantanal, natural grasslands, of excellent quality, feed an average of 3,000 cattle per square league during the dry season. The difficulty of raising horses in these damp lands makes it difficult to maintain the "*fazendas*".

The farmers founded the first villages on the banks of the swamp and have partly occupied it, despite the danger that floods mean to herds."

"In past centuries, the gold and diamonds of the mountains that border the N. the Pantanal were taken to the coast through it, to the Taquari, which flows there, to the Pardo, tributary of the Parana, the Tiete and Sao Paulo. Until 1736, the land road of Goias was not opened, travelled by mule caravans. The first trip through the Guapore-Mamore-Madeira to Para dates from 1742.

But soon it would be the Tapajoz who would absorb most of the Mato Grosso traffic. Salt was the main imported product. In the mid-nineteenth century Paraguay was open to international navigation, after bloody wars. Finally, in the middle of this century the Northwest railway was built, which arrives in Bolivia, but only serves the southern part of the Pantanal, it does not reach the Mato Grosso proper."

It would be necessary that the railroad that arrives from the coast to Brasilia and Goiania, extended to Cuiaba.

It seems, however, that this railway does not penetrate further into the interior because the navigation river along the Paraguai is sufficient for your needs. The problem is if, once the swamps were dried, this waterway would be maintained. If this were not the case, it would be necessary to extend those railway networks, which are transported faster but more expensive.

SIX

Here we find the eternal question. We cannot determine the viability of the project due to lack of precise data and specific knowledge. But there is something more important than all that: your need. If this project did not exist, it would have to be invented. It is not a colonization in the style of past times, in order to develop the resources of a territory or create a device of commercialized agriculture. The agriculture in these times that run (1984), before the excessive growth of the population, it has more peremptory purposes: the survival of the population and, by reflection, that of the State. The riches of Brazil are, rather, a mirage, an ornament: gold, diamonds, dye plants that gave it its name, spices. Under that there is a mass of 130 million (In 1984) who struggle hard with quite doubtful natural resources. A mountainous country, in some regions, jungle in others.

Open roads, build cities, break fields, obtain energy sources, everything is done with great effort, overcoming very considerable natural difficulties. The Brazilian masses hustle in large cities, fleeing from the inhospitable countryside, even though it is not precisely what is missing land.

It is not an emigration caused by the excess population of the rural territories, unable to feed it - this only occurs in the Sertao – but the very difficult of taking advantage of the land, the lack of agricultural land itself. The populated part of Brazil is a territory of ancient mountains, covered in much of jungle, abrupt, fragmented, rarely rich soil. Vegetation creates a false appearance of fertility.

But we well know that the tropical forest is a creation of itself, independent of the quality of the soil in which it is rooted. It is like a greenhouse in which vegetation sustains itself artificially through moisture and leaf debris. It is a work of millennia and when it is cut down, it never becomes as before. This balance is broken by breaking through the jungle and then the harsh reality is revealed: the soil that sustains it is rarely optimal for agriculture. This is the drama of Brazil. An immense country -17 times larger than Spain-, whose exuberance creates the illusion of a non-existent fertility.

But the population survives in limited spaces, tearing off resources that are not precisely those that promised their immensity and brilliance.

This is the reality of Brazil. It has to sustain a huge population with no exceptional resources. These things must be kept in mind. Because the Brazilians should not be the first fooled by this paradox. They must have a clear awareness of their reality. In 1979, agriculture provided only 11% of income, while industry 38% and services 51%.

Today Brazil (1984 data) is a country that lives from its industry, with a large population to support. It is precisely this industrial development the means by which the problem of population growth has been overcome.

However, this industrial development has reached its limit, has touched the ceiling, and this is an aspect of the issue that needs clarification.

SEVEN

Brazil's state and private debt abroad is 100,000 Mdl, equivalent to 1/3 of its annual product (1984 data).

In a time of great economic growth, this country could meet its growing needs, even if it was precarious. But the recession of recent years has sufficed so that its financial situation has gone bankrupt. This gives us an idea of the precariousness of this situation.

This country, which was developing a strong industrialization, has suffered strongly from the impact of the crisis and has not been able to withstand it.

Because that economic growth was forced, in a certain artificial way, in which one had to combine, on the one hand, the eagerness of great benefits of the financial groups and, on the other, the need to meet increasingly large social demands. However, there is no choice but to go one way or another; You can't take both at the same time. And doubting between these two possibilities has been taken full by the swell of the world economic recession, specifically by the industrial recession.

World industrial production has been stagnant for some years. But Brazil needs to produce more, sell more, to create jobs and sustain its growing population. Each year should generate a million new jobs. This should be provided by industrial activity, cities. But the world market is saturated, and it is not possible to continue growing at a strong pace as before. In conclusion, the urban economy cannot completely solve the problem and other solutions must be sought.

EIGHT

It is evident that the water of the San Francisco river could be diverted towards the coast of Recife and Natal, providing this rainy region for half a year with a water supply during the dry season. It is a more limited project, but of great importance for this overpopulated region, in which the drought has wreaked havoc. This region is covered with sugarcane crops. A strip of 50 km wide and 600 km long between the mouth of San Francisco and Cabo de San Roque; therefore, its extension is 30,000 km2.

It also seems absurd that such a simple solution has not been addressed, because the flow rate of San Francisco is 2,800 m3 on average; it would only be necessary to retain its waters from the rainy season to the dry one and use them in that plain now cultivated to obtain in it a second harvest.

No coastal obstacle would interrupt this channel. At the foot of the Paulo Alfonso waterfall (80 meters), the height is over 100 meters above sea level and from here the whole of this very low coastal plain is dominated.

This would be a complementary project. It would only be necessary to build a retention pond above the waterfalls and a 700 km channel below them. The thing being so clear and obvious, my mistrust is reborn: why has it not been done?

"The rains are abundant in the coastal strip, with totals greater than 2 ms, decreasing inland. They are distributed mainly from summer to autumn, while the dry season runs from July to December, with a minimum in September or October. Inside we find an increasingly arid region and more arid rains and more irregular rains.

The rains are always concentrated in a season (winter), which alternates with the dry season (verao or estiagem). But the so-called winter does not fall everywhere in the same months. Recife receives 58% of the rains in the four months from April to July; Fortaleza, 82; in the five from February to June. Thus, three rainfall regimes can be distinguished: autumn on the N coast, winter in the east and summer in the interior. These differences are explained by the wind regime in the immediate Atlantic region.

The proximity of different climatic zones, whose limits move capriciously from one side to another, causes an extreme irregularity of rainfall. This irregularity is a more serious evil than the amount of rain, relatively abundant. Frequently from one year to another the rains are double or half. In Rio Grande do Norte (Natal) the rains in 1915 were only 1/3 or 1/5 of those of 1914. Inside, they frequently appear in the form of local thrombus, with no general effect, while around the drought rages."

"In the coastal area, today almost completely broken, the wet forest originally extended. From this forest came the Brazil stick. The forests extended in rare points to more than 50 km of the coast and neither formed an absolutely continuous mass. The interior of the plateau is covered with xerophytic forest (adapted to drought)."

"The common limit of forest vegetation and deep decomposition soils runs a distance of 50 to 75 km from the coast; beyond the cattle region begins."

The diversion of the waters of San Francisco to the coastal plain, both to the North (to the end of San Roque) and to the S (to the Bay of Bahia) is something simple and perfectly feasible. The waters must be retained at the top and distributed by channels in the coastal plain. That's it.

NINE

The Paraguai River has its sources at about 500 ms altitude and a few km from them the town of Diamantino is only 300 ms high. About 250 km below and at the beginning of the Pantanal, the town of San Luis de Caceres is located at an altitude of 130 ms, which becomes 107 at the exit of it, at the crossroads of the Northwest railway. Between Corumba and Buenos Aires the horizontality of the channel is strange, the same between Corrientes (where Paraná and Paraguay meet) and Corumba than between Corrientes and Buenos Aires.

Horizontality is an important fact to take into account, but the breadth of the channel can be a determining factor to contain the flood and give it a way out. The 107 ms of Corumba are the essential data.

Actually, with that we enter into a much more general and complex problem: the regularization of the Silver network. The Mississippi is channelled, and also the rivers of China and Europe. On the other hand, those of the gigantic platense network run at will by the flat banks.

A work that, as time goes by, will have to rush by force is that of enclosing those rivers within artificial channels, which limit the flooding and give rapid exit to the water. In the case of the Paraguay River, Diamantino or Corrientes there is a distance of 2,500 km. The height of the city of Corrientes is 7 ms, but it is some distance from the river and above its flood. Resisrencia, capital of the Argentine province of Chaco, and also at the confluence of the two great rivers, is only 52 ms. Thus, if these data are accurate, the Paraguai River descends in the 1,500 km between the Pantanal exit and the Paraná mouth 55 ms, that is, 1 m./30 km, practically horizontals.

The Paraguay River has an average width of 350 ms: slow course with long sinuosities. Climb many meters during floods; just above the mouth, 6 ms have been measured on average. Then it stretches across the immediate plains. Asunción is located on a terrace that dominates the river from 5 ms; ships of 2.5 ms of draft can reach there. Asuncion is also of exceptional importance, from the point of view of river circulation, since its location is not accidental: the hills reach the river den this point exclusively and form a narrowing, called Angostura, in which the river only has 80 ms amplitude.

It is a point of great importance for this project, as the channel must be extended to avoid the overflow of the waters above.

TEN

Since we are dealing with the problems of Brazil in general, we have to consider the problem of dryland agriculture in the interior; that is, the crops that could be obtained from the rains if the soils allowed. If it is possible in the Sao Paulo region - the High Parana basin - why is it not in a series of high valleys: San Francisco, especially?

The San Francisco River has an almost flat central section of 1,300 km, where it only descends 100 ms. Here it forms an alluvial plain that reaches 20 km wide, which is flooded with floodwaters; It is covered with lagoons and covered by channels.

That is, exactly like the Araguaia and the Tocantins, although these run lower. Also the San Francisco is a river that needs to be drained in the region of the descent to the coast. In Pirapora, which is where the railroad crosses Brasilia, is 472 m. while in Juazeiro, at a distance of 1,300 km, it is 373 ms. In Jatoba, upstream of the waterfalls, it is at 298. Here the descent can not be more pronounced, because in the section of 130 km of the streams, it descends 280 m, so that in the Piranhas, which is 240 km from the sea, is only 18 meters above the sea.

This is a problem, because it is an excessively low height to be the source of a distribution channel along the coast; it would be necessary to build a pond that would raise the level of the river. The flood occurs late, at the end of the rainy season (from February to April); The level drops rapidly. The food in its middle course is quite poor.

On the other hand, the gigantic Amazon runs along a horizontal plain, but encased within it in deep ravines that isolate it from it, so that it has no opportunity to deposit its floods anywhere, except in its banks, which are dragged outwards.

Only in large areas of annual flooding can floods be deposited, but in the largest river, by far, in the world, there are hardly any; and on the coast it does not seem to advance either. It is a really extraordinary phenomenon, because the river flooding capacity at its mouths is an unequivocal symptom of the fertility of its lands. Rivers of low flow, like the Yellow, has managed to fill huge spaces in recent times.

This is a very interesting problem.

The Amazon drags thick sands up into the estuary. The Orinoco has a similar configuration and has managed to form a large delta. In the mouth the floods are not deposited but are dragged by the marine currents towards the N0, depositing in the coast of Guayana, between the Araguari and the Oyapoc. The lack of large deltas on the South American coast, except for the Orinoco, is due to marine action. First, the depth of the Atlantic coast. On the other hand, its huge floods, which reach 30 ms above the normal level.

On the other hand, the action of the tides, which is felt until Obidos, above the mouths of the Tapajoz and the Xingú. In the estuary of Pará the tide is 3ms and the flood is barely noticeable. The amplitude of the tides of sicigia (February-April) is 3.5 to 4 ms. The tides are very irregular and violent. The speed of these successive tidal waves can reach 20 km / h; they penetrate the mangrove-covered shorelines and river estuaries, where they produce pororoca. The enormous mass of the river fights against the tide, which forces it to retreat; the wave of tide moves upriver, fragmenting through canals and estuaries in waves of 4 ms of height with a rumble that is heard. The tidal wave advances upstream at a speed of 10 to 20 km / h. The material that starts the pororoca is dragged by the sea currents and thrown into the ocean. Upstream, the Amazon, is always an impetuous river due to the weight of its enormous body of water, So we find, then, that the Amazon flooding task is minimal, how could it be corrected? Only one way: stopping its course. Precisely in the narrowing of Obidos the main channel narrows to 1.8 km. at a great distance.

But can you really master this impetuous force that is sea rather than river? Their lands are a desert, as in the Sahara, but covered with water and plants. It seems that his destiny is to be the lung of the Earth. For something else it has no use.

ELEVEN

The case of Brazil is another phenomenon of developmentalism similar to that of India, in which mercantile and state interests are combined, trying to maintain a balance between social, state, a strong state, and mercantilist needs. But there has been an element that has significantly disrupted the financial situation: the demand for capital to finance the US state deficit. This has happened in recent years and of course, you should not talk logically.

Brazil has had to combine for several years the need to satisfy the desire for high profits of investors, the demands of a superabundant population (1984 data) and those of a State that needed to be strong. Brazil has become a considerable military power, the strongest in South America.

The States (about 24) have a great administrative autonomy, but the federal expenses are reduced to some matters. But not the maximum federal system, in which the central state is only responsible for military expenses and foreign policy direction.

Brazilian federalism is much more moderate, limited. But on this matter I have no details. Brazil is too big and heterogeneous. At any time and at a great distance, a conflict that would put the survival of the State in danger could erupt.

TWELVE

With regard to the drainage of the Paraguai River, it is clear that the only serious problem is to discharge the waters, by extending the channels, rather than deepening them. Set and expand the main channels to simply exit the water. That is the whole problem: expanding the channels, clearing them, giving way to the flood. With this simple file it will be possible to avoid the annual flooding of a territory of 80,000 km2, 8 Mhas.

What can you get with that? The food capacity of an intensely cultivated territory is very large.

It varies between 200 Hb / km2 and more than 500. Let's put between a minimum of 200 and a maximum of 600. As this region has a prolonged dry season, it would only give, in principle, a harvest, being able to maintain about 200 hb / km2, which multiplied by 80,000 give a food capacity for 16 million people. This seems insufficient for Brazil's food demand. But this is not the calculation, it is not appropriate. With 8 million hectares, if cultivated entirely of corn, at a yield of 3 tons per hectare, the production would be 24 Mtn. If rice were grown, a much more interesting thing, at a yield of 4 tons / ha, 30 Mtn of this cereal would be obtained.

In Spain, rice paddies yield 6 tons / ha and this region would produce no less than 48 Mtn. A very respectable figure. The proposal must be, then, to convert the Pantanal into a huge rice field, layer z of producing between 30 and 50 Mtn of food for basic consumption, this would be enough to ensure a daily ration of this product of between 200 and 400 grams to the entire population Brazilian. It is a theoretical calculation, but it allows us to represent what it means for that country. 100 grams of rice have 350 calories.

Therefore, it would supply between 700 and 1,400 calories a day to the entire current Brazilian population (1984), which is between 1 / 3.5 and 1/2 of what is essential for survival. This with the intensive cultivation of a territory that only represents 1/108% of the Brazilian total. That is to say, cultivating in this way the hundredth part of the territory, it would ensure between the third part and the half of the Brazilian food needs and practically the total consumption of cereals.

It's worth a try?

Currently (1984), Brazil produces about 8 Mtn of rice, 22 of corn, 2 of wheat. Thus, about 32 Mtn of tn of cereals. In this region they would widely double current production. But above all,

It would satisfy the food deficit widely and make it, perhaps, an exporter. Let us not forget that Brazil is forced today, to obtain foreign exchange and meet its international obligations, to export a portion of the food it needs for consumption. This is the situation and thus I would solve this serious problem.

THIRTEEN

Let's not forget that at the end of the century *(* Written in 1984 by the author)*, Brazil will have a population of over 200 Mhb. Unlike the Spanish-born America, the Lusitanian has remained united.

Brazil is triple the largest of the Spanish-speaking States (Argentina) and its population is almost double that of the most populous (Mexico).

Brazil is a large state organization, strongly unified, with a strong national feeling. Brazil is a giant, whose problems cannot be ignored.

With the financial situation it suffers, the future does not allow too much hope. But the population continues to grow and needs to be met. Until the end of this twentieth century many things can happen and it depends on the measures that are now adopted that these are bearable or tragic. A society cannot be subjected to unbearable pressure. If the previous situation was not good, the predictable one does not offer many doubts. Brazilian society cannot withstand the joint pressure of the economic crisis and population growth and must necessarily enter into a deep convulsion in a not too distant timeframe.

What can happen?

1984

<u>PROPOSAL</u>

HIGH PARAGUAI
AND
SWAMPS OF ARAGUAIA

HIGH PARAGUAI

"Sir. I submit for your consideration a proposal or suggestion that, if appropriate to reality, could help to mitigate to a certain extent the food deficit that you currently suffer (1984) in the Federative Republic of Brazil. It summarizes the following:

The swamps of the High Paraguai form a vast wasted area, covered with recent sediments. Annual flooding prevents them from being cultivated.

The proposal we make is to drain the swamps to cultivate an area of 8 million hectares. The slope is very small, and the drainage operation is difficult, but not impossible. The rocky outcrops on its way out, along with Corumba, contribute significantly to maintaining El Pantanal. By lowering the level of the riverbed and expanding its channels, the waters would have a better outlet and probably the marshlands of the Xaraas would not flood. An agricultural area comparable to that of Sao Paulo would be obtained.

Instead of being used for commercial crops, they could serve as a source of supply for food raw materials, rice, corn, etc.

If flooding were avoided, a harvest could be obtained during the rainy season. If the rivers that cause it were partly retained by the circle of mountains that surround the plain, water would be available for a second harvest during the dry season, or for uninterrupted cultivation.

The Pantanal retains the waters of the Paraguai River and causes it to lose large flows by evaporation.

A complementary project to this could be the diversion of these waters, once the flooding is prevented, on the one hand, and the evaporation, on the other, in the territory of Paraguay and Argentina, towards the interior of the Chaco, below the level of the 100 meters above the sea, for irrigation of the great southern plains.

If, for example, rice were grown exclusively, at a yield of 4 tons per hectare (in many regions - such as here in Valencia - 6 tons are obtained) the food yield of the region would be 32 million tons, more than what Brazil needs right now (1984 data), but less than what you will need at the pace of a generation.

This gives us an idea of the food capacity of the small territory.

If this were possible - with the means at my disposal, I cannot know and I also do not know if any project has already been considered -, Brazil would have a firm food base on which to sustain itself in the immediate future and avoid the rugged consequences that arise Of not having it. With this wish I send you the suggestion, to which, if feasible, there is no doubt that the excellent Brazilian engineering will know how to take advantage."

WAMPS
OF
ARAGUAIA

"Sir. I submit for your consideration a suggestion regarding the agricultural use of the Araguaia River:

As is known, the Araguaia forms in its middle course an extensive swampy region of almost 400 kilometres along the river, with an average width close to 100 kilometres. Its extension is 3 to 4 million hectares.

Over the ages the river has deposited its floods there, creating a large potentially agricultural space, covered by flooding.

The first question that assails us is whether the floods deposited by the Araguaia in that territory are fertile or are formed by sands and other sterile materials. From here and with the data I have it is impossible to know. But if these floods were fertile as a whole, Brazil could gain for its food supply a very large cultivated space, capable of large productions.

The proposal that I suggest consists in facilitating the exit of the stagnant waters of the Araguaia, retained by the obstacles that the river has to cross below. For this, it would be enough to carry out a drainage operation, extending and, above all, deepening the river channels, so that the floodplain would be free for cultivation.

If this territory were fertile and could be easily emptied, and rice was cultivated, for example, 15-20 million tons of this food could be obtained from it, considerable assistance to the State's demands.

In addition, the colonization of the territory, located 500 kilometres northwest of Brasilia, would mean a great step forward in the process of occupying the semi-empty spaces of the interior. If its colonization were possible, several million people could stay in the territory and such inhabited nucleus would serve as an intermediate point between traditional Brazil and the Amazon. It all depends on the fertility of the soils, which, unfortunately, is not possible to verify.

Perhaps, in their eagerness to take full advantage of their agricultural spaces, they have already considered and discarded this possibility. But, if it had not been so, I would be very glad that this suggestion may be useful."

Página del autor en Amazon:

Amazon.com/author/juansanzsanz

Página del autor en Smashwords:

**https://www.smashwords.com/profile
/view/juansanzsanz**